STA... ...PORT

Swimming

Rebecca Hunter

Photography by Chris Fairclough

W

FRANKLIN WATTS
LONDON • SYDNEY

First published in 2008 by
Franklin Watts
338 Euston Road
London NW1 3BH

Franklin Watts Australia
Level 17/207 Kent Street
Sydney NSW 2000

ISBN: 978 0 7496 7835 7

Dewey classification number: 797.2' 1

A CIP catalogue record for this book is available from the British Library.

Planning and production by Discovery Books Limited
Editor: Rebecca Hunter
Designer: Ian Winton
Photography: Chris Fairclough
Consultant: Denise Hazelwood, ASA Full teacher level two, UKCC Expert
witness assessor, UKCC Certificate in tutoring sport, RLSS Pool lifeguard.

The author, packager and publisher would like to thank the following
people for their participation in this book: the staff and children at the Flash
Leisure Centre, Welshpool, Wales.
Badges and certificates on pages 22-23 supplied by the Amateur Swimming
Association.

Printed in China

Franklin Watts is a division of Hachette Children's Books,
an Hachette Livre UK company
www.hachettelivre.co.uk

Contents

The swimming pool

Swimming is not just a sport. There are many reasons why you should learn to swim: it is good exercise, a lot of fun and it may even save your life one day.

Most people learn to swim in a swimming pool at a sports centre. Many centres have several pools of different depths and some have fun features such as **flumes** or a wave machine. The main pool has lines on the bottom, marking out lanes that people can swim up and down.

Safety in the pool

Water can be dangerous so it is important to act sensibly and safely in the pool. Young children should not swim unless they are with an adult.

All pools have a **lifeguard** on duty. They have a whistle that they can blow if people are running or misbehaving.

Pen Dwfn
Deep End
1.8m
DIM DEIFIO
NO DIVING

Look for signs telling you which end of the pool is the deep end. If you are not a strong swimmer, do not swim out of your depth. Only dive in water more than 1.8m deep. This warning sign is also written in Welsh.

7

Swimming equipment

You do not need much equipment to swim. Swimming kit consists of swimming costumes for girls and swimming trunks for boys. Both are made of thin, stretchy material. This means you can swim easily through the water.

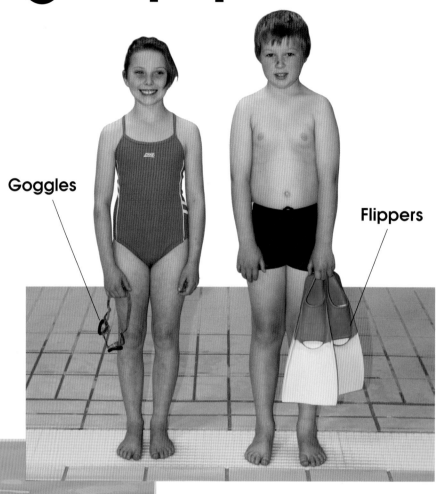

Goggles

Flippers

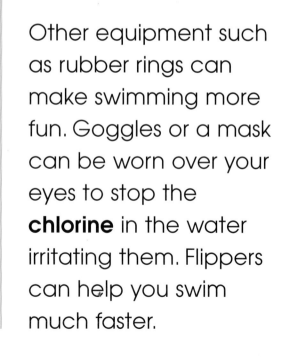

Other equipment such as rubber rings can make swimming more fun. Goggles or a mask can be worn over your eyes to stop the **chlorine** in the water irritating them. Flippers can help you swim much faster.

Swimming aids

Young children often learn to swim using armbands. They give them confidence by keeping them afloat.

If you can swim but need a little help sometimes, floats are a good idea.

Swimming with a float can allow you to practise your leg movements or breathing skills.

Entering the water

There are several ways to get into a pool. You should choose the one you feel happiest with.

Young children, or anyone who is slightly nervous, should enter the pool backwards down the steps. This gives you something to hold onto until you are right in the water.

1

The swivel entry (left) is another way to get in the water safely and easily.

2

1. Start by sitting on the edge of the pool. Place your hands on the side edge to one side of you.

2. Twist your body round and lower it into the pool, while still holding onto the edge.

Jumping

If you are a very confident swimmer, and don't mind going under water, you may prefer to jump into the water. Don't 'bomb' or splash other swimmers.

1. Make sure you have a clear area of water to jump into, and that it is deep enough.

2. Jump a good distance into the pool so you don't touch the side.

Blowing bubbles

To become a good swimmer you will need to be able to swim with your face in the water. To become confident at this, you should practise blowing bubbles in the water. Take a deep breath then blow out slowly.

Floating and sculling

Swimming really only involves two skills: floating, and moving through the water. Learning how to float easily is the first important skill to learn.

Floating

It is often easiest to learn to float on your back first. Take a deep breath to fill your **lungs** with air. Then spread your arms and legs out into a star shape. This shape creates the most

buoyancy in the water. Knowing how to float on your back well is an important skill to have in an emergency. It allows you to rest and breathe in deep water.

Treading water

If you need to stay in one place in the water for any length of time, you will need to 'tread water'. Your body should be upright in the water and you should move just enough to stop you sinking. Make wide, slow movements with your hands under the water and move your legs slowly backwards and forwards.

Sculling

Sculling is a combination of floating and moving. Start in the back-float position. Your arms should move out, away from your body and then back towards it. At the same time your hands should be moving in a figure-of-8 pattern.

Sculling is a relaxing way to float in the water. Try and keep your legs together!

Gliding

Gliding is done by pushing off from the edge of the pool, and then floating without moving your arms and legs. Gliding can be done on the front or back.

Breaststroke

Breaststroke is the stroke you are most likely to learn first. It is an easy and comfortable stroke to swim. However it can be hard to make the legs and arms work together correctly.

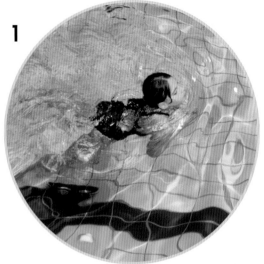

This sequence shows the arm movements of breaststroke.

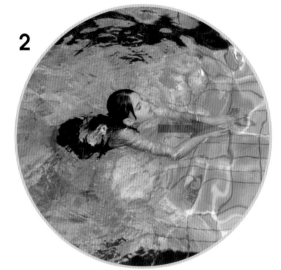

1. Hold your hands together and up against your chest under your chin.

2. Push your arms forward and glide for a moment with your hands flat near the surface of the water.

3. Turn your hands so that your palms face outwards, and pull your arms apart and through the water, ending up with your hands in their original position, against your chest.

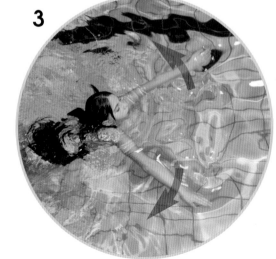

Breastroke legs

The leg movements for breaststroke are a bit like the actions of a frog! You can practise while holding on to the edge of the pool. Start with your legs straight out behind you. Bend your legs and bring your feet up under your body.

Kick your legs out to the side. Then streamline your body by bringing your legs together and pointing your toes. You should be gliding forward at the same time (see step 2, opposite).

Front crawl

Front crawl is probably the most popular stroke and the fastest. In a **freestyle** race, when any stroke can be used, most people pick the front crawl. This is why crawl is often also known as freestyle.

In crawl the arms move in a windmill motion opposite each other, while the legs kick up and down. You should remain horizontal in the water and stretch each stroke out as much as possible. A strong kick will keep your legs from sinking behind you.

Front crawl arms

1. Bring your right arm out of the water, elbow first, behind you by your right side.

2. Cup your hand and move the extended arm over your head until it enters the water again in front of you.

Front crawl legs

Your legs just move up and down. They should be close together with loose, floppy ankles. The kick should not make a big splash, but should just gently move the surface of the water. You can practise leg movements with a float to help you.

3. As you draw your right arm through the water beneath your body your left arm will be coming out of the water.

Breathing

To start with you can do the crawl without putting your face in the water. When you are ready, you will have to learn how to breathe in water correctly. Take a breathe on one side by turning your head to that side as the arm comes out of the water (see step 1, opposite).

Backstroke and butterfly

Backstroke is similar to the front crawl but is done on your back.

1. Start by floating on your back while kicking your legs up and down. Keep one arm straight as you raise it out of the water from your waist to a fully extended position.

2. Keep your legs straight. Your arm should travel past your ear and re-enter the water behind your head.

3. As one hand enters the water, the other hand should be leaving it. Try to keep your fingers together!

Single arm pulling

You can practise your arm actions with a float. Hold the float in one hand while using the other arm to do the backstroke.

Butterfly

Done properly, the butterfly stroke is a smooth, gliding stroke, but you may find it difficult and tiring to learn.

1. Lift your head up and pull both arms out of the water. Swing both arms together in a circular movement forwards.

2. Your head and arms should re-enter the water together in a diving motion. Your body should glide for a moment after your arms enter the water.

Butterfly legs

To do the butterfly legs you need to pretend your legs are glued together. You should move from the hips. The overall action is a bit like a dolphin.

It is a good idea to practise the kick with flippers on to get the feeling of the power of the kick and to move through the water more easily.

Diving

Once you are happy with jumping into the water, you will probably want to improve your **technique** and learn to dive in.

1. Stand on the edge of the pool with your toes curled over the edge. Bend over and try to put your hands by your toes.

2. Move your hands back to your hips ready to swing forward. Try to dive into the water about 1 metre from the edge.

3. Push off and enter the water with your ears between your arms and your hands flat and together. Try to keep your feet together!

In competitive swimming, swimmers start their races from dive stands. Swimmers should hold onto the front of the stand. They should stand with one foot forward and one foot back – a bit like the starting position for a running race.

When the starter blows the whistle they push off with both feet and dive as far forward into the water as they can.

Races and competitions

Racing

Once you are a confident swimmer you will probably want to take part in races and competitions.

Breaststroke, front crawl and butterfly races can start in the pool in this position (right), or with a dive (see page 21).

A race is won when a person touches the edge of the pool with their fingertips (below).

A backstroke race always starts in the pool. The swimmers either hold on to the pool edge or, as in this case (right), the racing stands.

Relays and medleys

A relay is a race that has several teams of usually eight people: four at each end of the pool. Each swimmer swims one length of the pool and when they touch the edge the next team member dives in. The first team to have all members finish is the winner.

A medley is a race that involves all four of the swimming strokes. In an individual medley each swimmer has to swim the four strokes in this order: butterfly, backstroke, breaststroke, freestyle.

In a medley relay a team of swimmers cover the four swimming strokes in the following order: backstroke, breaststroke, butterfly, freestyle.

In this picture of a relay, the nearest swimmer is doing front crawl while the swimmer behind him is doing the backstroke.

Awards and badges

There are several swimming plans that you can follow. These will train and test you and award you badges and **certificates** when you have achieved each of the levels.

The Amateur Swimming Association (ASA) has a new National Plan that starts with easy tasks for non-swimmers and ends with swimmers being able to swim 1,500m.

The 7-stage plan

Stages 1 and 2 are for non-swimmers and are about gaining confidence in the water. Swimmers may wear armbands or use floats.

Stages 3, 4 and 5 involve gliding, sculling and swimming without help. By the end of stage 5 swimmers should be able to swim 10 metres in each of the four strokes.

Stage 6 includes swimming with proper breathing. Swimmers also have to be able to swim 10m with their clothes on.

By the end of stage 7 swimmers should be able to tread water for 30 seconds, perform a sitting dive, swim 50m in each of the strokes and swim 200m continuously in one stroke.

After the first seven stages, levels 8-10 allow you to take part in different types of **aquatic** activities. **Water polo**, diving, **synchronised** swimming and lifesaving are some of the options available to you.

Water safety

Swimming is a great form of exercise and a good way to have fun. However safety is very important in the pool area.

Always make sure there is a responsible adult watching you.

If you are not a strong swimmer make sure you swim within your depth. Don't run around the pool, and don't dive in the shallow end. If you are having a lesson always listen carefully to what your instructor is saying.

On the beach

It is great to have a day out on the beach, but remember although the sea looks shallow and calm, it still can be dangerous.

Always swim in the safe area on a beach. Most beaches are watched by a lifeguard who will be able to see you if you get into trouble. If you are in difficulty, stay calm and try and attract someone's attention.

Raise one arm to signal for help and shout loudly. If you have an **inflatable** toy or boat to hold onto, stay with it. You will be seen more easily and you won't get so tired. When you have attracted someone's attention, float on your back and try to breath normally, while they come to your rescue.

Glossary

aquatic anything relating to water.

buoyancy the ability to stay afloat in water.

certificate a piece of paper that shows you have reached a certain level in a subject or sport.

chlorine a chemical that keeps water clean.

flume a large water slide.

freestyle a competition in which you can use any stroke.

inflatable something that can be filled with air.

lifeguard a person who is an expert swimmer and trained in first aid. Lifeguards work at swimming pools and on the beach.

lungs the organs in your body that help you to breathe.

synchronised doing something at the same time as somebody else.

technique using skills to do something in the best way possible.

water polo a game a bit like volley ball that is played in a pool.

Further reading

Know Your Sport: Swimming, Clive Gifford, Franklin Watts, 2008

Sporting Skills: Swimming, Clive Gifford, Hodder Wayland, 2008

How to Improve at: Swimming, Ticktock Media Ltd, 2005

Swimming: Steps to Success, David G. Thomas, Human Kinetics Europe Ltd, 2005

Superguides: Swimming, Rick Cross, Dorling Kindersley, 2000

Further information

It is easy to get started in swimming. To find out more you can contact your local leisure centre or the Amateur Swimming Association.

Amateur Swimming Association (ASA)
Harold Fern House
Derby Square
Loughborough
Leicestershire
LE11 5AL
Website: www.britishswimming.org

Australian Sports Commission
PO Box 176
Belconnen
ACT 2616
Australia
Website: www.ausport.gov.au

Swimming Australia Ltd
12/7 Beissel Street
Belconnen
ACT 2617
Australia
Website: www.swimming.org.au

Index

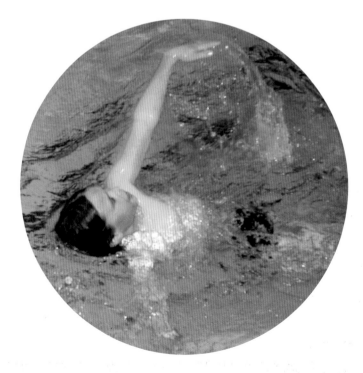